10/17/17
18.95

American Government

POLITICAL PARTIES

John Perritano

D0890497

AMERICAN GOVERNMENT

Foundations
Office of the President
Congress
Supreme Court
Political Parties

Photo credits: Page 12/13: Everett Historical / Shutterstock.com; page 20/21: Charlotte Purdy / Shutterstock.com; page 22: Joseph Sohm / Shutterstock.com; page 26: Everett Historical / Shutterstock.com; page 27: Joseph Sohm / Shutterstock.com; page 42: Everett Historical / Shutterstock.com; 51: Joseph Sohm / Shutterstock.com; page 55: Olga Popova / Shutterstock.com; page 70: Olga Popova / Shutterstock.com; page 82: Rob Crandall / Shutterstock.com; page 83: Alamy.com

Copyright © 2016 by Saddleback Educational Publishing. All rights reserved. No part of this book may be reproduced in any form or by any means, electronic or mechanical, including photocopying, recording, scanning, or by any information storage and retrieval system, without the written permission of the publisher. SADDLEBACK EDUCATIONAL PUBLISHING and any associated logos are trademarks and/or registered trademarks of Saddleback Educational Publishing.

ISBN-13: 978-1-68021-122-1
ISBN-10: 1-68021-122-6
eBook: 978-1-63078-437-9

Printed in Guangzhou, China
NOR/0216/CA21600249

20 19 18 17 16 1 2 3 4 5

3 4873 00532 0536

TABLE OF CONTENTS

We the People
of the United States, in Order to form a
Article. I
Section. 1. All legislative Powers herein granted shall be vested in a Congress of the United States

Introduction

The United States Constitution is over 225 years old. It says nothing about **politics**. Not a word about political parties. Why? It didn't have to. People knew who the first president would be. It was a fact. George Washington. No political parties needed. Everyone got along. Or did they? Then Washington retired ...

Leaders were ready to fight. Would people like the Constitution? Some wanted a strong central government. Others wanted the states to lead. The groups were called factions. Political parties were born.

What is a political party? A political party is a group of people. They have the same ideas. People work together to win elections. They want to control the government. Why? So their ideas can be put into action. There are two main parties. The Democratic Party. The Republican Party. They compete for power. Each wants to win. Parties help us know what **candidates** stand for. Some say they make it easier to vote.

There have been six party systems. What's that? A label. It describes the history of American politics. One party dominated each of the six eras. Party ideas change over time. Things happen to alter people's thinking. People switch parties.

1. 1790s–1820s. Federalists vs. Democratic-Republicans. 1796 was an election year. John Adams vs. Thomas Jefferson. Adams won. He became president. Four years passed. Time for another election. People gave speeches. The **campaign** was ugly. Each side insulted the other. Jefferson won. His party ruled. Adams's party faded away. The Federalists were gone. Only one party was left.

2. 1820s–1850s. Democrats vs. Whigs. Jefferson's party split. There were many groups. The Democrats was one. Another was the Whigs. Four men ran for president in 1824. It was a big mess. There was a tie. Congress had to decide. John Quincy Adams was named president. Andrew Jackson won in 1828. People called him a king. Party members met. Meetings were called **conventions**. Campaigns used sayings. Called **slogans**. They were catchy. But war was coming.

3. 1850s–1890s. Democrats vs. Republicans. Many did not like slavery. It ended the Whig Party. The Republican Party was born. Abraham Lincoln was its candidate. He became president. The country went to war. 750,000 men died. Slavery ended. The South was rebuilt. It was expensive. And it took time. People lost interest. Republicans left the South. **Jim Crow** laws were passed. They were unfair to people of color. The country grew. People emigrated, 25 million of them.

4. 1890s–1930s. Democrats vs. Republicans. Republicans were pro-business. They won elections. No Democrat won until 1912. Third parties formed. They rarely won elections. But Americans liked some of their ideas. The two main parties liked them too. They adopted them. Working conditions improved. Child labor laws were passed. Women got the right to vote.

5. 1932–1968. Democrats vs. Republicans. The stock market crashed. Workers lost their jobs. Shops closed. Banks failed. Democrats won in 1932. Franklin D. Roosevelt became president. He had plans to help. It was called the New Deal. The government grew. It spent money. Other presidents followed. The War on Poverty. The Great Society. Those were Democratic programs. They cost trillions.

6. 1968–now. Democrats vs. Republicans. Split government. Nobody agrees. Working together is not easy. Are we in a new era? Some say yes. Others say no. It happened in 1968. The South voted Republican. The Midwest too. Republicans today don't want too much government. Democrats like social programs. Who will win on the next Election Day?

A house divided against itself cannot stand.

—Abraham Lincoln

CAMPAIGN SLOGANS	
William Henry Harrison, 1840	Tippecanoe and Tyler Too
Abraham Lincoln, 1864	Don't Swap Horses in the Middle of the Stream
Calvin Coolidge, 1924	Keep Cool with Coolidge
Herbert Hoover, 1928	A Chicken in Every Pot and a Car in Every Garage
Franklin Delano Roosevelt, 1932	Happy Days Are Here Again
Dwight D. Eisenhower, 1953	I Like Ike
Jimmy Carter, 1976	Not Just Peanuts
Ronald Reagan, 1984	It's Morning Again in America

TEDDY

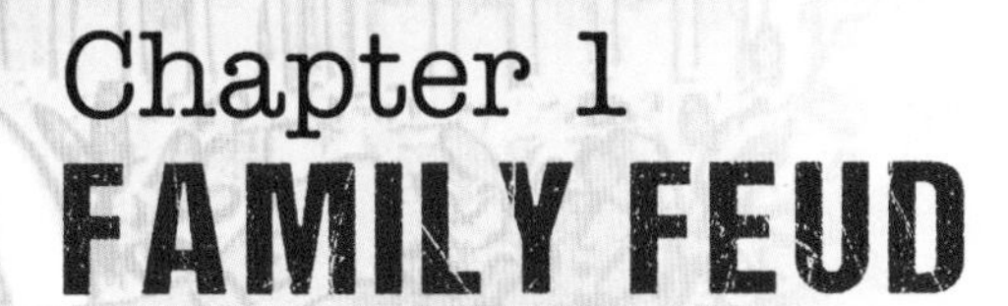

Chapter 1
FAMILY FEUD

Theodore Roosevelt and William H. Taft were good friends. They belonged to the same political party. A political party is a group of people. They have the same ideas. Working together, they win elections.

Both Taft and Roosevelt were Republicans. Roosevelt was the U.S. president. In 1904, he picked Taft to be secretary of war. Taft was loyal to Roosevelt. He supported Roosevelt's ideas. Roosevelt left office in 1909. Voters picked Taft as president. Roosevelt was happy. He thought Taft would continue his **policies**.

Theodore Roosevelt

Roosevelt was all smiles when he left the White House. He went hunting in Africa. The former president said he would never return to politics. Roosevelt came back from Africa. He saw Taft ignoring all he had done. Roosevelt felt let down. He wanted Taft out of office.

Roosevelt took on his one-time friend. He wanted to be the Republican choice for president in 1912. One of them would face-off with a Democrat on Election Day. His name was Woodrow Wilson. He was a member of the Democratic Party. Wilson was the governor of New Jersey.

Think About It: *Does America need political parties?*

[CRAZY CONVENTION]

Roosevelt and Taft were loyal to their party. They each asked for the party's support. Republican Party members met in Chicago. Members were called delegates. They held a convention. It was to pick the party's candidate for president. Some wanted Taft. Others wanted Roosevelt.

Party members yelled. They fought. The party was split. Taft or Roosevelt? Roosevelt or Taft? In the end, the delegates picked Taft. Roosevelt was angry. He and his followers stormed out of the meeting. They left the Republican Party. A new party

Symbol of Progressive Party

was formed. It was called the Progressive Party. The newspapers called it the Bull Moose Party. Roosevelt once said he was as strong as a bull moose.

[THE RACE WAS ON]

The race for president was on. It was a three-way contest. Taft against Roosevelt. Both against Wilson. A Republican battling a Progressive. Both wanted to win over a Democrat.

All three parties had ideas. The Republicans wanted to tax imports. Goods coming into the U.S. would be taxed. The Democrats thought states should have more power. The federal government should have less power. The Progressives wanted women to vote. They could not at the time. The party also wanted workers to earn a minimum wage.

Roosevelt's friends were mad at the two main parties. They didn't like that the parties were afraid of change.

The new party's leaders had good ideas. They thought the other parties had ignored important issues. Those parties weren't looking out for the people. "They have become the tools of corrupt interests," the Progressives said.

[FATHEADS AND RADICALS]

The election was rough. Roosevelt called Taft names. He said Taft was a "fathead with the brains of a guinea pig." Taft said Roosevelt and his friends were "radicals." The Democrats were happy. Voters usually choose

Theodore Roosevelt campaigning

candidates from their own party. They wanted Roosevelt in the race. The Democrats knew it would split the vote. Republicans would be torn. Neither Taft nor Roosevelt would win. Wilson would become president.

That's exactly what happened. Some Republicans voted for Roosevelt. Others voted for Taft. No one had enough votes to beat Wilson.

The Progressive Party didn't last very long. It disappeared by 1916. The Republicans are still around. So are the Democrats. They are the two main political parties in the U.S. Smaller parties exist too. They all fight one another on Election Day. Parties want to win elections. They want people to like their ideas. Their goal is to control the government.

FACES IN THE CROWD

Thomas Nast
Born: September 27, 1840
Died: December 7, 1902

The symbol of the Republican Party is an elephant. The symbol of the Democratic Party is a donkey. They were the work of Thomas Nast. Nast worked for *Harper's Magazine*. He drew political cartoons. They are drawings printed in newspapers and magazines. Political cartoons had power. They made tough issues easy to understand. Political cartoons still appear in print today.

It was 1870. Nast drew a cartoon. The image was of a donkey. It kicked a dead lion. Democrats were meant to be the donkey. The lion was Abraham Lincoln's former secretary of war. The man had just died. The drawing showed how Democrats were shaming Lincoln. "A live jackass kicking a dead lion." Those words were below the cartoon. The donkey was forever linked to the Democratic Party.

Nast once drew an elephant. It called out Republicans. The elephant was running toward a pit of "chaos." Nast implied the party was afraid.

Chapter 2

PARTY ON

It was 100 years after Roosevelt fought Taft. Things were quiet in the Republican Party. Party members met in 2012. They would pick a presidential candidate. There was a meeting. It was in Tampa, Florida. No one walked out. No one started a new party. Republicans stood together. They picked Mitt Romney. He was once governor of Massachusetts.

The Democrats were united too. They held their meeting a few weeks later. It was in Charlotte, North Carolina. The Democrats picked a candidate. It was President Barack Obama. Presidential elections are held every four years.

People from each party spoke for their candidate. The parties raised money. They held meetings. Parties paid for political ads. Rock stars got into the act too. Kid Rock sang songs for Romney. Bruce Springsteen held concerts for Obama. Neither candidate could be elected without their party's support. Campaigns cost money. Candidates need to hire expert staff. They need **media** attention. Political parties give money. They attract smart people. And the media tends to report major party news.

Think About It: *Are political parties a good thing for democracy?*

[FACTIONS]

Political parties are not part of the Constitution. That's because people were worried about them. George Washington was one. James Madison was another. They called them "factions." A faction is a small number of people. The people do not agree with the larger group. Both men said political

George Washington

parties could harm the country. They would make the government weak.

Yet political parties exist now because of the Constitution. Why? Two-thirds of the states had to approve the document. States had to agree with it. Some people did not agree. They wanted states to have more power. The central government should be weaker, they said. Others were for it. They wanted a strong central government.

The U.S. Constitution

From that fight, two groups formed. One was the Federalists. They agreed with the Constitution. The central government should be powerful. Washington and Madison were Federalists. So was Alexander Hamilton.

Another group was the Anti-Federalists. They had another view. The Constitution gave the government too much power. Each party tried to change people's minds. The Federalists won. The Constitution became the law of the land.

[HERE TO STAY]

Political parties were here to stay. At first, there were two. There were Federalists. Hamilton led them. There were Democratic-Republicans. Thomas Jefferson led them. The party was against kings and queens. That's why they chose their name. The party was for individual rights. The Democratic-Republicans thought states should have all the power.

Alexander Hamilton

Thomas Jefferson

Years passed. It was before the Civil War. Political parties grew stronger. Some came and went. Others stayed for a long time. Each had a cause. There was the Whig Party. It did not like President Andrew Jackson. People called him "King Andrew." He took more power for himself. Jackson got rid of the national bank. There was the Free-Soil Party. It did not want slavery in new areas. The American Party was **anti-immigrant**. They were called the Know-Nothings. All of those parties are gone. Most people today are Republicans or Democrats.

[PARTY GOALS]

What is the main goal of a political party? To run the government. Parties want to pass new laws.

Those laws show their ideas. It doesn't matter what government they run. It could be local or national. Parties must win elections to do this. Each finds candidates for elected office. These candidates have to share the party's views and goals. Once it wins, a political party has power. Its members work together to pass new laws. They also change old laws.

Political parties keep an eye on each other too. They speak out on what they believe in. One party often thinks the other party is wrong. They will make sure the other party follows the law. Party leaders keep close watch on who's in charge. They will often criticize elected officials from the other party.

[THIRD PARTIES]

Democrats and Republicans get a lot of attention. But they are not the only political parties. Voters can join other national parties. These are called third parties. Today there are five third parties in the U.S. They include the Green Party. The Constitution Party. The Libertarian Party. The Natural Law Party. And the Reform Party.

Sometimes third party candidates can change an election's result. That's what the Progressives did in 1912. Some say that also happened in 2000.

FACES IN THE CROWD

Ralph Nader

Born: February 27, 1934

It was 2000. Ralph Nader ran for president. He belonged to the Green Party. It believes in many things. The environment should be protected. Workers should be treated fairly. Nader ran against the two main candidates. One was Al Gore. He was a Democrat. The other was George W. Bush. He was a Republican.

Nader got a big share of the popular vote. In that election, Gore received more popular votes than Bush. But Bush won the vote in the Electoral College. The college is not real. It is a group of people. Members are called electors. Each state has members. They meet after Election Day. There is a vote for president. In most states, winning the popular vote wins that state's electors.

The election results in Florida were key. Who would win its electoral votes? Some said Nader took votes away from Gore. He split the Democrats. Bush barely won Florida. People said it was because of Nader. He did not agree.

[CONGRESS AND PARTIES]

Political parties control how Congress works. Congress is the lawmaking part of government. It is called the legislative branch. Members of Congress make laws. Congress has two houses. One is the Senate. The other is the House of Representatives. Each house has a majority party. That is the party with the most members. Each house also has a minority party. That is the party with the fewest members.

Each party in Congress elects its own leaders. There are leaders for the House and Senate. They build support for bills. Bills might become laws. They organize votes. Leaders plan **strategy**. They also pick people to serve on committees.

ON THE JOB

It's important to get things done. Lawmakers in all parties have to come together. Many times they do not. Party loyalty often runs politics. Parties don't like to make deals. Especially if it's an issue members care deeply about. A tax increase is one issue. Military spending is another. Workers' rights is a third. But there are many more.

Sometimes parties *do* come together. It's for the good of all. Parties work out their differences. In 2014, Congress agreed on a law. It was called the Workforce Innovation and Opportunity Act. The law helps people learn new job skills. It lets them gain on-the-job experience. The law passed the House 415–6. The Senate voted 95–3. It was a great show of cooperation.

Chapter 3
HOW POLITICAL PARTIES WORK

Political parties serve individuals and groups. A person may want to join a political party. Why? Because they agree with the party on most issues. People care about many things. Some care about lowering taxes. Others care about helping the poor. A party helps people put their thoughts into words. In turn, people vote for candidates that they agree with. Political parties make it easy for voters. Candidates don't keep their ideas a secret.

But no one is made to join a party. People don't have to pay dues. They don't have to go to meetings. They simply register to vote. There are many ways to do this. People can fill out forms. They are called voter registration forms. Forms can be found at many public offices. People can even register to vote at the DMV. There are 23 states that offer online registration too. You can find out more at *usa.gov*. People can then pick a party. But only if they want to join. They don't have to. Many people don't join a party. They are often called Independents.

Interest groups help political parties for other reasons. Interest groups are people that share the same views. The National Resources Defense Council is one. It is an environmental group. Interest groups might help small businesses. Teachers. Or farmers. Each is concerned about a specific issue. Teachers often support a political party. They might pick one for its views on education. Small businesses might support a party for its views on taxes.

Interest groups help elect candidates. They raise money. Buy TV ads. Volunteer on Election Day. Help voters get to the polls. They can hold meetings. Meetings urge people to support a candidate.

Think About It: *Do political parties help favored candidates win the nomination? Is the primary process fair?*

[ORGANIZED]

Big political parties are highly organized. Each has levels of organization. There is the national level. They have paid workers. But there are also state and local chapters. Many volunteers help the party. All work with the same goal in mind. They want to win as many elections as possible.

A political party has many parts. There are **precincts**. But there are also **wards** and committees. All are the lowest levels of a party. They are called the **rank and file**.

Each major party has a national committee. It is made up of people from each state. Each committee also has a staff. There are volunteers too. The committee's job is to get people elected to national office.

[PRECINCTS]

There are election precincts. Government officials set them up. Precincts are the smallest. They may only have a few voters. Sometimes they are called districts. Each has at least one polling place. That's where people go to vote. A poll could be at a school. It could also be at a library or a firehouse.

Each party picks a precinct captain or some other leader. The captain is a link. They connect voters with the party. They talk to people. Leaders have one goal. They want people to vote for their party's candidates.

[WARDS AND COUNTY COMMITTEES]

Wards include many precincts or districts. Most wards are numbered. Each ward has members that sit on the party's county committee. These people can be elected. Or party members pick them. This happens at a local meeting. Higher party officials can also pick them.

County committees are the next highest level. A chairperson runs them. That person has a lot of power.

[STATE COMMITTEES]

State committees are large. Their top job is to elect people to state offices. The biggest office is the governor. Others are state treasurer and state senator. But there are many more. Each party decides who is on the state committee.

Some parties elect committee members. This happens in Connecticut. Republicans and Democrats do this. Candidates in the same party want the same job. People vote to pick the person.

Some parties choose committee members another way. It is at a meeting. Party members take a vote there. Nebraska Democrats select their committee this way.

ON THE JOB

Groups can run political parties. Sometimes they are called political machines. It's not a real machine. A group or a "boss" controls how people vote. The group does favors for people. That's how it works. It might help a person find a job. The group might help a business owner get a permit. In return, people vote for party candidates.

Tammany Hall was a powerful political group. Democrats in New York City ran it. The group controlled city government. In the 1800s, it helped many of the city's poor. It gave them food, jobs, and homes. The group also gave jobs to its supporters. This is known as the spoils system. It often broke laws to keep itself in charge.

The machine went on for years. In 1966, a Republican mayor was elected. The group lost power for good.

[NATIONAL COMMITTEE]

National committees lead the party. They are at the top of the organization. State committees work with national ones. Their goal is to get candidates elected. It could be to Congress. The top job is the presidency.

One is the Democratic National Committee (DNC). It has more than 200 elected members. The DNC is also made up of chairs and vice chairs. The chairs come from state committees. The DNC was formed in 1848.

The other is the Republican National Committee (RNC). It has 168 members. Members are from each state and U.S. territory. Each has three representatives on the committee. The RNC began in 1856.

A chairperson runs both national committees. The national committee members elect them.

Each committee also has staff. They work to help candidates for office get elected. Volunteers also help run the committees.

National committees raise money. They make plans. The committees also hold a national meeting. The meeting is every four years. It's called a convention. There, candidates for president and vice president are officially chosen.

[PLATFORMS]

Parties are not focused on one candidate. They have a set of ideas. It is called a **platform**. A platform is what the party believes. The party's candidate wins an election. Then the party can try to change laws.

1912 Progressive Party convention in Chicago, where the goal was to create the party's platform.

In 2012, the Republicans had ideas. They wanted the government to change. The Democrats had ideas too. They wanted more banking laws. These ideas were their platforms. Both were published online and in print. Everyone could read them.

State committees have ideas for candidates in state elections. National committees have them for national candidates. These candidates generally agree with their party's thinking. But they are mostly led by their own views on an issue. The platform is supposed to guide the actions of elected officials.

FACES IN THE CROWD

Thomas Pendergast
Born: July 22, 1872
Died: January 26, 1945

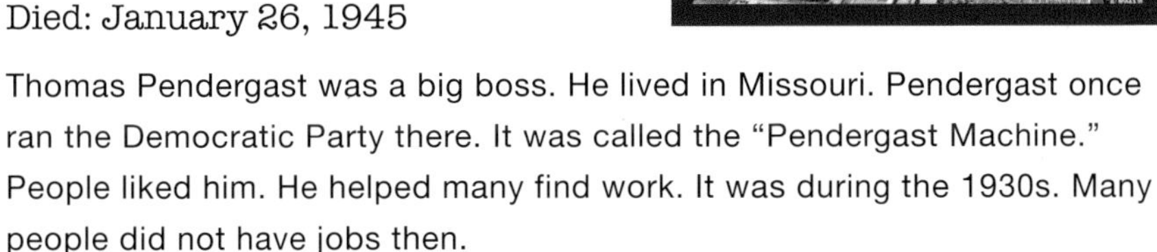

Thomas Pendergast was a big boss. He lived in Missouri. Pendergast once ran the Democratic Party there. It was called the "Pendergast Machine." People liked him. He helped many find work. It was during the 1930s. Many people did not have jobs then.

Workers and their families showed their thanks. How? By voting for candidates Pendergast liked. One was Harry S. Truman. He ran for judge in 1922. Truman won. Pendergast also helped him become a U.S. senator. Truman later became president. Pendergast was dishonest. He used his power for his own good. The boss broke the law. He did not pay his taxes. Pendergast went to jail for one year.

LAKE SUPERIOR
L. MICHIGAN
Chippewas
Menomonies
Sioux
Winnebagoes
Prairie du Chien
Milwaukie
Galena
Chicago
Peoria
SPRINGFIELD
INDIANAPOLIS
Vandalia
Council Bluffs
Omahaws
Pawnees
Otoes
Sacs & Foxes
Sacs & Iowas
Kickapoos
Delawares
Kanzas
Shawnees
Independence
JEFFERSON CITY
St. Louis
Missouri R.
Potawatamies
Osages
Creeks
Seminoles
Choctaws
Canadian R.
Red R.
Fayetteville
Van Buren
Ft. Smith
LITTLE ROCK
Helena
Arkansas
Washington
Millersburg
Natchitoches
Memphis
NASHVILLE
FRANKFORT
Louisville
Huntsville
TUSCALOOSA
Montgomery
Columbus
JACKSON
Vicksburg
Natchez
Mobile
Pensacola

Chapter 4
REPUBLICANS

It was 1854. The issue was slavery. African Americans were slaves. They were bought and sold. Families were broken up. Africans were kidnapped. Europeans brought them to the colonies. They forced them to work. The first slaves landed in Jamestown, Virginia. The year was 1619.

The Northern states slowly ended slavery. But slaves were important to the South. Slaves worked on big farms. They helped grow crops. Things like cotton, tobacco, and sugar cane. Slavery kept the profits high for white owners.

Slavery split the Democrats. Northern party members wanted slavery gone. They did not want new states to have slaves. Slavery should be unlawful in new areas. Southern party members accepted slavery. They wanted slavery to grow as the country grew.

In 1854, anti-slavery groups came together. They formed a political party. The new party had some Northern Democrats. They met in Jackson, Michigan. Congress should not allow slavery in new states, they said.

Horace Greeley

At the time, Horace Greeley owned a newspaper. It was in New York. He gave the party its name. He said "Republican" was a good name for the party. Why? Because it defended freedom. It was simple. People knew what it meant.

Think About It: *Does government work best when it is divided?*

[PARTY OF LINCOLN]

It was 1856. The Republicans had their first candidate for president. He was John C. Frémont. Frémont was an explorer. He'd been a U.S. senator from California. Frémont lost. Democrat James Buchanan won. Two years later, many issues split the country. Four major parties came on the scene. There were Northern and Southern Democrats. Republicans. And the Constitutional Union Party.

The next Republican candidate was Abraham Lincoln. He was the first Republican elected president. It was during the 1860 election. Southerners believed Lincoln and his party

Detail of Lincoln campaign banner

would end slavery. Lincoln's election sparked the Civil War. The war lasted four years. Then slavery was gone for good. It was 1865.

FACES IN THE CROWD

Thaddeus Stevens
Born: April 4, 1792
Died: August 11, 1868

In 1865, Andrew Johnson became president. He was a Democrat. President Johnson made a plan. The plan was to unite the country. There was a hitch. The Southern states did not have to help ex-slaves. The states passed "black codes." They were laws that harmed African Americans. Some laws took away rights. Some put limits on freedom. Black people could not sit on a jury. They needed permission to travel. In some states, blacks could not own land. They could not rent a house.

Congress was against the president's plan. There were more Republicans. One Republican leader was Thaddeus Stevens. He was a congressman from Pennsylvania. Stevens was against slavery. He did not like the way Johnson ran things. Stevens helped pass new laws. The laws gave ex-slaves more rights. He also led Congress to get rid Johnson. He wanted Johnson out of office. The president was impeached. He was found not guilty. It was only by one vote. He stayed in office until 1869.

[IN CHARGE]

Republicans held power after the war. The army kept order in the South. How would Southern states re-enter the Union? The party set up rules. It supported small businesses and farmers. Republicans passed laws. They gave African Americans more rights. Ex-slaves now had the right to vote. African Americans wanted to join the party.

Many blacks were elected to office. They were Republicans. Joseph Rainey was from South Carolina. He was elected to Congress. Rainey was the first black man to serve in the House. He did so in 1869. A year later, Hiram Revels joined him. Revels was the first black senator. The senator was from Mississippi.

Joseph Rainey

Hiram Revels

[GOOD TIMES]

Between 1876 and 1892, elections were close. The two parties were both strong. Neither party was on top. Republicans paid less notice to the South. Their focus was on businesses and banks. The party wanted the economy to grow. It was in favor of high taxes for imports.

In 1897, William McKinley became president. He was a Republican. Many Americans liked what he said. He stood for working people and business leaders. The president was serving a second term. His vice president was Theodore Roosevelt.

McKinley was killed. Roosevelt became president.

Republicans would be the top party for many years. The party helped the U.S. become a world power. In 1908, President Theodore Roosevelt sent navy ships around the world. He wanted to show that the country was strong. Roosevelt also helped end a war. It was between Russia and Japan.

It was 1919. Republicans helped women get the right to vote. Congress passed the 19th Amendment. Five years later another law was passed. President Calvin Coolidge signed it. Native Americans were now U.S. citizens.

America was doing well. The economy was strong through the 1920s. The Republican Party's ideas made people money. Voters liked how the party ran things. They kept the party in power. After 1896, Republicans had won all but two presidential elections. In 1929, they also controlled Congress.

[THE GREAT DEPRESSION]

Then the stock market fell. It was 1929. The price of stocks dropped fast. People sold them at low prices. They had paid much more. Millions saw their money gone. It took only minutes.

The Great Depression followed. People lost their

jobs. They also lost their homes and farms. Business owners closed their shops. Banks failed. Factories closed. Savings accounts were wiped out.

The Republican Party was still in charge. President Herbert Hoover tried to fix the mess. But he wanted the government to have a limited role. Meddling would harm business, he thought. Government rules could take away freedoms. Hoover also didn't want to put the government in debt. He tried to help people at the local level. The president asked for private help too. But he was not successful.

People grew tired. They wanted change. Most Americans voted against Hoover. The midterm elections were coming. The Republican Party lost control of Congress.

[THE NEW DEAL]

Franklin D. Roosevelt

In 1933, the Democratic Party took over. Franklin D. Roosevelt was the new president. He made plans. Created programs. The programs put people back to work. It was called the New Deal.

One project was the Works Progress Administration. Millions of Americans were given jobs. They built roads, bridges, and airports. Roosevelt died in 1945. His vice president took over as president. Harry S. Truman served for eight years.

Democrats had been in power for 20 years. But it was coming to an end. Republicans did not like the way the Democrats were running things. President Truman thought the government should get people jobs. He wanted more civil rights laws. Truman wanted health care for all. It was part of his Fair Deal. Many opposed the plan. They wanted the government to back off. Congress said no to most of the Fair Deal.

Dwight D. Eisenhower

In 1953, a Republican was elected. He was Dwight D. Eisenhower. He carried on many of the plans set by the Democrats before him. Eisenhower didn't want to overspend. He worked for a balanced budget. There was some progress in the area of civil rights. The president signed a civil rights bill. Called the Civil Rights Act of 1957. It protected the voting rights of African Americans.

[CIVIL RIGHTS]

World War II had ended. For the next 20 years, people worked to pass civil rights laws. The two parties both helped. They got a civil rights bill passed through Congress. Called the Civil Rights Act of 1964. It made it illegal to treat people unfairly.

Some people didn't like mixing races. They were against equal rights for blacks. Third parties formed. The American Independent Party wanted separate but equal. The States' Rights Party was also in favor of it. Southern Democrats had created it.

In 1968, another campaign started. The two main

parties didn't talk about race. Some Democrats felt their party had let them down. Before 1948, they felt their party respected states' rights. It supported Southern values. Some joined the Republican Party.

By the end of the 1960s, the South had become the center of Republican power. As of 2015, the party controls seven states. Those states used to be Democratic. Texas is one. Louisiana is another. The others are Alabama, Georgia, and Mississippi. Plus North and South Carolina.

SOUTHERN STATES WITH A REPUBLICAN MAJORITY

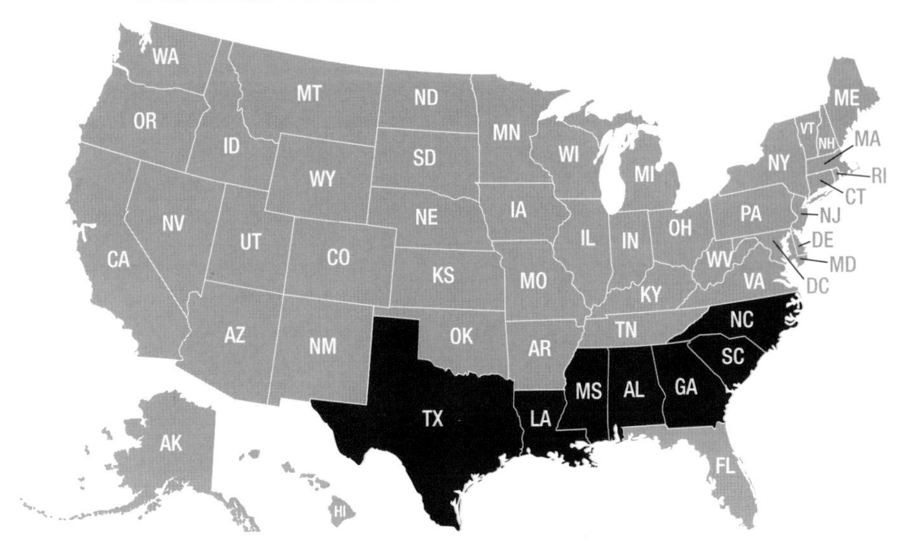

[NO TO BIG GOVERNMENT]

Many of today's Republicans are **conservative**. The party honors American traditions. They have strong views on the economy. They want it to be healthy. The party believes in keeping people safe. It wants a strong military.

Republicans say they offer the "maximum economic freedom." Freedom makes it possible for success. The party believes in self-discipline. It also believes in hard work. People succeed because they work hard. Government should not be in people's business. People should rely on themselves.

ON THE JOB

Republicans are often called "right wing." This is because they have conservative views. They want limited government. Democrats are often called "left wing." This is because they have liberal views. They want government to help people. Where did "right" and "left" come from?

Let's go back to the French Revolution. In 1789, the French overthrew their king. It was a bloody time. A new government took over. It was the National Assembly. It included members of several parties. Those who wanted big change sat on the left. Those who wanted less change sat on the right.

Chapter 5
DEMOCRATS

The Democratic Party is the other major political party. It is the oldest party in the U.S. Its roots go back to 1792.

Do you remember the Federalists? What about the Anti-Federalists? The Constitution became law. The Federalists ran the government. George Washington was the party's first president. John Adams was its second. The party wanted a strong central government.

In 1792, a new party was born. It was the Republican Party. Don't confuse it with the modern Republican Party. It began during the Civil War. The two are not the same. The Republican Party of the early 1800s was different. It is a distant cousin to today's Democrats.

Think About It: *Are the two main political parties too radical?*

[JEFFERSON AND HIS PARTY]

Thomas Jefferson

Thomas Jefferson was an Anti-Federalist. He believed in people's freedom. States' rights were important to him. He did not want a strong central government. Jefferson and others formed the Republican Party. It is also known as the Democratic-Republicans. The party didn't like the Federalists. It kept watch. Checked their power.

The two parties did not agree on much. Jefferson's party wanted France to be a friend. The Federalists did not. They didn't want ties with France. Britain was better liked. They thought it would be a better ally.

War broke out. It was the end of the 1790s. Britain and France fought. John Adams agreed to a harsh set of laws. They were called the Alien and Sedition Acts. The acts were a group of four laws. Three were focused on non-U.S. citizens. The other punished Americans who disagreed with the government.

People could not criticize their leaders. The laws made Adams unpopular. They went against the rights every American expected.

Congress of the United States,
begun and held at the City of New-York, on
Wednesday the Fourth of March, ... and seven hundred and eighty nine.
THE
RESOLVED
ARTICLES

The laws were bad for Adams. His place in history was ruined. Years later, Adams was sorry he'd agreed. But it was too late. Tempers rose. Voters got mad at the party in power. The Federalists lost. Jefferson became president in 1800. His party was in power for years. Jefferson fired many of the Federalists working in government. By 1820, the Federalist Party was gone. That made Jefferson's party the only one in the country.

HISTORY HAPPENED HERE

Event: Hamilton–Burr Duel

Who: Alexander Hamilton and Aaron Burr

When: July 11, 1804

Alexander Hamilton was a Federalist. Aaron Burr was a Democratic-Republican. He was also the vice president. The two men did not like each other. Burr's term as vice president was ending. He ran for governor of New York. Hamilton was from that state. He told people not to vote for Burr. Burr's bid failed. He blamed Hamilton for the loss.

At a dinner, Hamilton said something bad about Burr. Word got back to Burr. He dared Hamilton to a duel. A duel is a fight with guns. At the time, dueling was a common way to settle disputes.

Burr hoped the fight would help his political career. The day of the duel came. It was held in Weehawken, New Jersey. Each man fired a shot. Burr was okay. Hamilton was hurt. He died the next day. The bullet ended Burr's career. He was charged with murder. Burr never held elected office again.

[SPLIT PARTY]

By 1824, the Democratic-Republicans split. Each side picked its own candidates for president. There were four of them. John Quincy Adams was one. Andrew Jackson was another. William H. Crawford and Henry Clay were two others. No man won enough electoral votes to become president. That meant the House of Representatives had to decide. Who would be president? House members picked Adams. Adams got 13 votes. Jackson got 7. And Clay, 4.

John Quincy Adams

Adams was president. But the party was still torn. Jackson was popular in the South and West. His followers were simply called "Democrats." The name was from Democratic-Republicans. It was the 1828 election. Jackson beat Adams this time. The party's official name became Democrat.

In 1834, the U.S. had a second major party. It was the Whigs. They didn't like Jackson or the Democrats. Why? Because they didn't agree with Jackson's ideas. They thought he acted like a king.

The Democrats won most elections for almost 30 years. By the late 1850s, the party was split. Members disagreed on slavery. Northern Democrats didn't like it. Southern Democrats did. Their fighting led to the new Republican Party taking control. It was under the leadership of Abraham Lincoln and others. By this time, the Whigs and some smaller parties disappeared. Many joined the Republicans. After the Civil War, Democrats and Republicans were the main political parties.

[POWER IN THE SOUTH]

The Civil War ended. Many Democrats lived in the South. They did not like the way Republicans ran things. Republicans passed laws. Those laws helped ex-slaves. Schools were built. The Republicans made sure blacks could vote. The army kept order in the South. Federal laws were enforced. The time was called **Reconstruction**.

Reconstruction ended in 1877. Then the Democrats took power in the South. They passed laws that hurt African Americans. The laws became known as "Jim Crow." Jim Crow was a character. An actor created him in the 1830s. The actor painted his face black. He made fun of African Americans. But the stories go back further than that. There was a song called "Jump Jim Crow." Crows were tricksters in West African stories. There was one called Jim. Slaves brought the tale to America. Only later did the name become linked with racism.

Unfair laws caused terrible suffering. It was not legal for blacks to eat in the same restaurants as whites. Blacks could not testify in court. Jim Crow laws stopped African Americans from voting. The laws stopped them

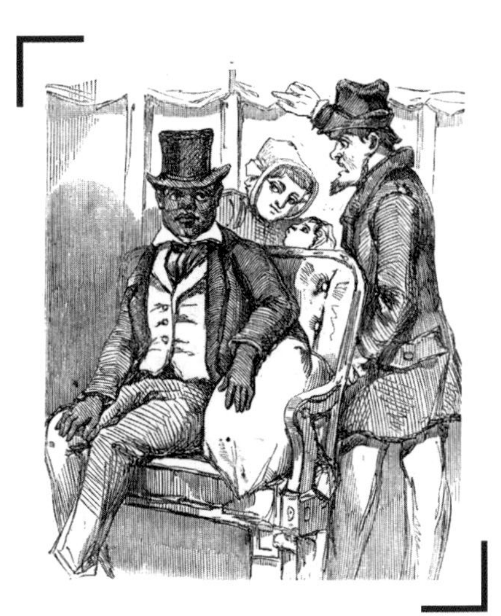

from getting a good education. The Democratic Party was known as the "white man's party" then. They didn't like Republicans for supporting African Americans.

Republicans ruled politics from 1897–1932. Then Woodrow Wilson became president. He won against two other men. William H. Taft and Theodore Roosevelt ran in 1912 too. They lost. The Democrat moved into the White House.

[BACK IN CHARGE]

Things changed in the 1930s. It was during the Great Depression. Voters blamed the Republicans. They said the party did not do enough. It didn't help people find jobs. Democrats were back on top. Leading them was Franklin D. Roosevelt (FDR). He was the fifth cousin of Theodore Roosevelt. FDR became

Franklin D. Roosevelt

president in 1933. He changed the Democratic Party forever.

Roosevelt's family was rich. Still, he believed many people needed help. FDR thought government should help. He came up with a plan. It was called the New Deal.

The New Deal created over 30 agencies. The Civilian Conservation Corps was one. And the Civil Works Administration was another. Those and other offices put people to work. The government passed new rules. Those rules were for banks. They also affected the stock market. People who couldn't find work got help. Roosevelt

Social Security poster

also created Social Security. He wanted people to have a **safety net**. This meant having retirement money. It helped people when they were too oldto work.

Because of Roosevelt, many people became Democrats. Factory workers and farmers joined the party. So did African Americans and immigrants. Many others supported the president. They elected him four times.

[A FAIR SHOT]

The Democratic Party is the oldest ongoing party in the country. Today the party has millions of members. Many Democrats are **liberal**. They are not against new ideas. Democrats support social change. The party has a central belief. It is based on the idea that Americans are better together than on their own. The party values hardworking families. It looks out for them.

Democrats believe everyone should get the same chances. They call this getting "a fair shot." The party believes in fairness. The poor should have the same opportunities. There shouldn't be different rules for different groups of people.

ON THE JOB

The DNC chair is a woman. Her name is Debbie Wasserman Schultz. She was elected to Congress in 2004. The House member is from Florida. She represents parts of two counties. They are Miami-Dade and Broward. Wasserman Schultz became DNC chair in 2011.

Chapter 6
TIME FOR A CHANGE?

Ever heard of Thomas Hoefling? What about Merlin Miller? Virgil Goode? Jill Stein? Rocky Anderson, Gary Johnson, or Peta Lindsay? Don't feel bad. Most people don't know them. All ran for president in 2012. They were members of third parties. Third parties represent many voters. These voters don't like the two major parties. They don't agree with Democrats or Republicans. Voters can't see themselves as either.

The U.S. has three branches of government. Each branch shares power. There are many other kinds of government. In Canada and Britain, a leader is picked from a group of lawmakers. So is the cabinet. They all make laws. And they all enforce them. Our founding fathers did not want that. Nor did they want the majority to rule. All states had to share power equally.

NUMBER OF ELECTORS IN EACH STATE

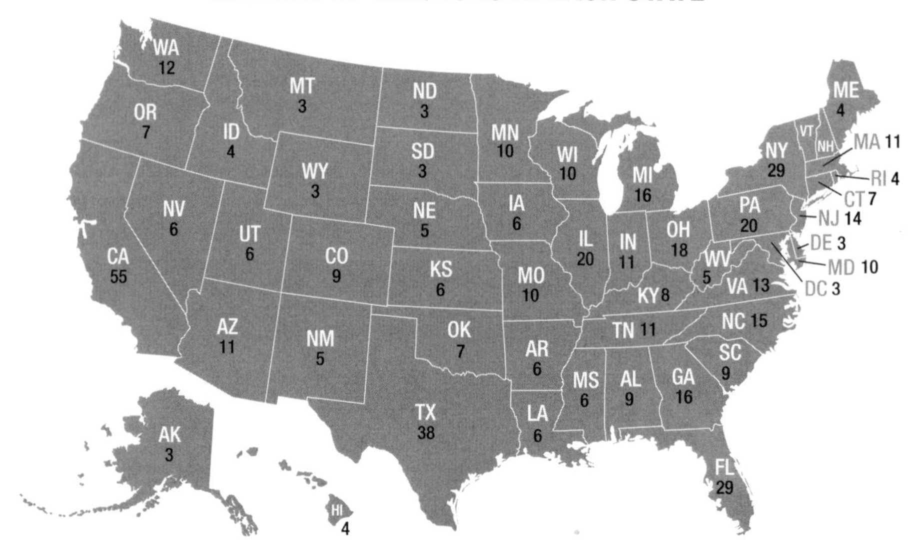

The Electoral College was set up. It makes third parties impossible. Why? A total majority by a third-party candidate can't happen. It's because of **electors**. The popular vote does not say who the next president will be. Electors do. And candidates have to win enough states. That way they will win the most electors. In 1992, candidate H. Ross Perot won 19 percent of the popular vote. But he didn't win any electors.

Two parties rule in the U.S. Those parties have gained enough power to run things. It wasn't always this way. The country used to have many parties. Third-party candidates took on top-party candidates all the time.

That changed after the Civil War. Democrats and Republicans passed laws in each state. The laws kept third parties small. They couldn't get too big. Those laws made it hard for other candidates to get on the ballot. In a way, the two parties fixed the game in their favor.

Today third parties tend to get lost in the mix. That's because the two major parties get the most attention. The news media usually ignores third parties. Third-party candidates are rarely invited to political debates. Third parties don't raise as much money either. The whole process is "like climbing a cliff with a slippery rope." That's what Ralph Nader once said.

Think About It: *Is the two-party system bad for America?*

[BAD?]

Many say a two-party system is bad. There was a poll in 2014. It showed that 71 percent of Independents thought the U.S. needed a third party. And 47 percent of Democrats agreed. So did 46 percent of Republicans. They said America is a mix of people. Two parties cannot be all things to everyone.

2014 POLL ASKS, DOES THE U.S. NEED A THIRD PARTY?

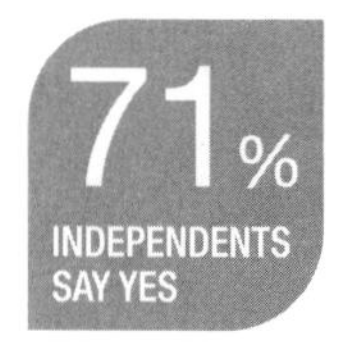

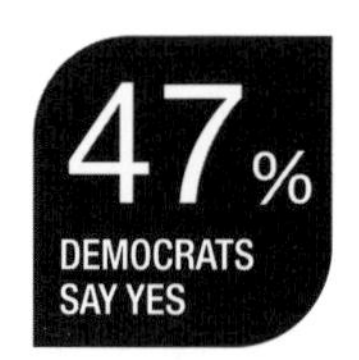

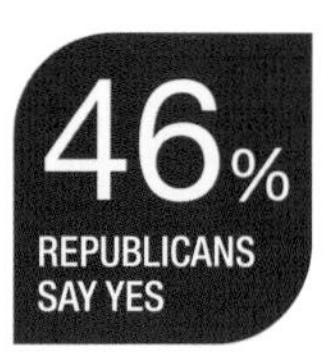

Voters often get mad. Why? Because there is a lack of choice during elections. Some say Republicans and Democrats are frozen in their beliefs. They won't work together to get things done. Each party naturally goes against the other. Politicians have to defend the thinking of their party. They do this even though it might be wrong.

Sometimes that works against them. It can hurt them with the people they represent. People might get mad at them. When that happens, people change their vote. The politician will not win the next election. They will lose their job.

Money plays a big role too. Many say major party candidates are for sale. Rich people give to their campaigns. What if their candidate gets elected? Donors might ask for favors. They might want support on an issue.

Third parties can sway government. They can bring issues to the public's attention. The modern Republican Party was once a third party. It formed over the issue of slavery. Slavery was later abolished. Theodore Roosevelt's Progressive Party supported women's rights. A few years later, women won the right to vote. In both examples, third parties have helped the country. The direction changes at important times.

[GOOD?]

Not so fast, others say. Yes, the two big parties rule. It's true that they often argue. Sometimes nothing gets done. Yes, they represent special groups and people. But many believe the two-party system is good for the country.

Third parties, some people say, weaken one major party. At the same time it makes the other stronger. Then what happens? People get more divided. Things cannot get done.

That's what happened in 1912. It was Election Day. Theodore Roosevelt and the Progressives split the vote. A Democrat won. The election weakened the Republicans for eight years. They lost the presidency twice. The Democrats were able to set the agenda. They passed laws they wanted. Democratic lawmakers started the Federal Trade Commission. They began an income tax. The Republicans couldn't stop them.

Do third parties represent large groups of people? People say no. Most third parties have narrow views. Look at today's Justice Party. It is based on ending corporate influence in politics. Many third parties don't force the major parties to be any better.

ON THE JOB

Political parties form for many reasons.

- The Anti-Masonic Party (1828–1832). It was the first third party in the country. Members were against the Freemasons. It was an organization of men. The party held a convention. It was the first party to do so. This party was also the first to let people know what it stood for.

- The American Vegetarian Party (1947). It was anti-meat. Dr. John Maxwell was the party's first presidential candidate. Maxwell was 84 years old at the time. He hadn't eaten meat in 45 years. The party continued until 1963.

- The O.W.L. Party (1976). It was formed in a jazz club in Tumwater, Washington. OWL stood for "Out with Logic." And "On with Lunacy." Its motto was "We don't give a hoot!" Party members got on the ballot in Washington. State lawmakers then changed the rules. They made it harder for third parties to get noticed.

FACES IN THE CROWD

H. Ross Perot

Born: June 27, 1930

H. Ross Perot was a businessman. He started a third party. It was called the Reform Party. He said the two-party system did not work. Most people think he split the Republican vote. President George H. W. Bush was running for reelection. He lost. The split let Democrat Bill Clinton become president. Neither Clinton nor Bush talked much about overspending. Then Perot entered the race. Government spending became a hot topic.

[PEOPLE CONNECT]

There are 320 million Americans. The country is over 3.8 million square miles. Our nation is the third largest in the world by land mass. By population we are third too.

How do people in such a large place talk with their leaders? How do they connect? Elected lawmakers are key. They link us to the government. Political parties connect us to ideas. They help us understand the issues. We elect leaders because we agree with them. Democracy depends on sharing ideas.

People identify with political parties. They call themselves Democrats. Or Republicans. Or even Independents. We show our interests through political parties. They help people get more involved in government. People have a voice. Voters make choices on Election Day.

The morality of a [political] party must grow out of the conscience and the participation of the voters.

—Eleanor Roosevelt

GLOSSARY

anti-immigrant: people who are against others who come to their country to live there

campaign: an action plan with a goal in mind

candidates: people who are trying to get elected to office

conservative: a person or group who favors traditional values and is cautious about change

convention: a large meeting where people come together to make decisions

elector: a member of the Electoral College

interest group: an organized group of people who try to influence government for a particular cause

Jim Crow: a group of laws that treated African Americans unfairly

liberal: a person or group who favors new ideas and believes government should support change

media: communication via television, radio, newspapers, magazines, and the Internet

platform: a public statement made by a political party that says what they stand for

policies: a plan with goals

politics: the activities of the government, lawmakers, and political parties, especially the disagreements among parties who have or want to have power

precinct: a part of a town or city that is divided for voting purposes

rank and file: the ordinary members of a group, not including leaders or officers

Reconstruction: the years following the Civil War when the federal government controlled the South

safety net: protective government programs that help people in tough times

slogan: a short saying that is easy to remember

strategy: a plan that involves setting goals

ward: a part of a city that is divided for voting purposes and contains more than one precinct

PRIMARY SOURCES

[A LOOK AT THE PAST]

What is a primary source? It is a document. Or a piece of art. Or an artifact. It was created in the past. A primary source can answer questions. It can also lead to more questions. Three primary sources are included in this book. **The Preamble to the U.S. Constitution**. It explains why the framers chose to create a republic. **The Bill of Rights**. It guarantees certain freedoms. And the **Declaration of Independence**. It stresses natural rights. More can be found at the National Archives (online at *archives.gov.*) These sources were written for the people. (That means us.) The people broke free from the king's tyranny. The United States of America was born. Read the primary sources. Be an eyewitness to history.

We the people of the United States, in order to form a more perfect Union, establish justice, insure domestic Tranquility, provide for the common defense, promote the general welfare, and secure the blessings of liberty to ourselves and our posterity, do ordain and establish this Constitution for the United States of America.

[PREAMBLE]

THE U.S. BILL OF RIGHTS

THE PREAMBLE TO THE BILL OF RIGHTS

CONGRESS OF THE UNITED STATES begun and held at the City of New York, Wednesday, March 4, 1789.

THE Conventions of a number of the states, having at the time of their adopting the Constitution, expressed a desire, in order to prevent misconstruction or abuse of its powers, that further declaratory and restrictive clauses should be added: And as extending the ground of public confidence in the government, will best ensure the beneficent ends of its institution.

RESOLVED by the Senate and House of Representatives of the United States of America, in Congress assembled, two-thirds of both Houses concurring, that the following Articles be proposed to the legislatures of the several states, as amendments to the Constitution of the United States, all, or any of which articles, when ratified by three-fourths of the said legislatures, to be valid to all intents and purposes, as part of the said Constitution; viz.

ARTICLES in addition to, and amendment of the Constitution of the United States of America, proposed by Congress, and ratified by the legislatures of the several states, pursuant to the fifth article of the original Constitution.

AMENDMENT I

Congress shall make no law respecting an establishment of religion, or prohibiting the free exercise thereof; or abridging the freedom of speech, or of the press; or the right of the people peaceably to assemble, and to petition the government for a redress of grievances.

AMENDMENT II

A well regulated militia, being necessary to the security of a free state, the right of the people to keep and bear arms, shall not be infringed.

AMENDMENT III

No soldier shall, in time of peace be quartered in any house, without the consent of the owner, nor in time of war, but in a manner to be prescribed by law.

AMENDMENT IV

The right of the people to be secure in their persons, houses, papers, and effects, against unreasonable searches and seizures, shall not be violated, and no warrants shall issue, but upon probable cause, supported by oath or affirmation, and particularly describing the place to be searched, and the persons or things to be seized.

AMENDMENT V

No person shall be held to answer for a capital, or otherwise infamous crime, unless on a presentment or indictment of a grand jury, except in cases arising in the land or naval forces, or in the militia, when in actual service in time of war or public danger; nor shall any person be subject for the same offense to be twice put in jeopardy of life or limb; nor shall be compelled in any criminal case to be a witness against himself, nor be deprived of life, liberty, or property, without due process of law; nor shall private property be taken for public use, without just compensation.

AMENDMENT VI

In all criminal prosecutions, the accused shall enjoy the right to a speedy and public trial, by an impartial jury of the state and district wherein the crime shall have been committed, which district shall have been previously ascertained by law, and to be informed of the nature and cause of the accusation; to be confronted with the witnesses against him; to have compulsory process for obtaining witnesses in his favor, and to have the assistance of counsel for his defense.

AMENDMENT VII

In suits at common law, where the value in controversy shall exceed 20 dollars, the right of trial by jury shall be preserved, and no fact tried by a jury, shall be otherwise re-examined in any court of the United States, than according to the rules of the common law.

AMENDMENT VIII

Excessive bail shall not be required, nor excessive fines imposed, nor cruel and unusual punishments inflicted.

AMENDMENT IX

The enumeration in the Constitution, of certain rights, shall not be construed to deny or disparage others retained by the people.

AMENDMENT X

The powers not delegated to the United States by the Constitution, nor prohibited by it to the states, are reserved to the states respectively, or to the people.

IN CONGRESS, JULY 4, 1776.

The unanimous Declaration of the thirteen United States of America,

When in the course of human events, it becomes necessary for one people to dissolve the political bands which have connected them with another, and to assume among the powers of the earth, the separate and equal station to which the laws of nature and of nature's god entitle them, a decent respect to the opinions of mankind requires that they should declare the causes which impel them to the separation.

We hold these truths to be self-evident, that all men are created equal, that they are endowed by their Creator with certain unalienable rights, that among these are life, liberty and the pursuit of happiness. That to secure these rights, governments are instituted among men, deriving their just powers from the consent of the governed. That whenever any form of government becomes destructive of these ends, it is the right of the people to alter or to abolish it, and to institute new government, laying its foundation on such principles and organizing its powers in such form, as to them shall seem most likely to effect their safety and happiness. Prudence, indeed, will dictate that governments long established should not be changed for light and transient causes; and accordingly all experience has shown, that mankind are more disposed to suffer, while evils are sufferable, than to right themselves by abolishing the forms to which they are accustomed. But when a long train of abuses and usurpations, pursuing invariably the same object evinces a design to reduce them under absolute despotism, it is their right, it is their duty, to throw off such government, and to provide new guards for their future security. Such has been the patient sufferance of these colonies; and such is now the necessity which constrains them to alter their former systems of government. The history of the present king of Great Britain is a history of repeated injuries and usurpations, all having in direct object the establishment of an absolute tyranny over these states. To prove this, let facts be submitted to a candid world.

He has refused his assent to laws, the most wholesome and necessary for the public good.

He has forbidden his governors to pass laws of immediate and pressing importance, unless suspended in their operation till his assent should be obtained; and when so suspended, he has utterly neglected to attend to them.

He has refused to pass other laws for the accommodation of large districts of people, unless those people would relinquish the right of representation in the legislature, a right inestimable to them and formidable to tyrants only.

He has called together legislative bodies at places unusual, uncomfortable, and distant from the depository of their public records, for the sole purpose of fatiguing them into compliance with his measures.

He has dissolved representative houses repeatedly, for opposing with manly firmness his invasions on the rights of the people.

He has refused for a long time, after such dissolutions, to cause others to be elected; whereby the legislative powers, incapable of annihilation, have returned to the people at large for their exercise; the state remaining in the mean time exposed to all the dangers of invasion from without, and convulsions within.

He has endeavored to prevent the population of these states; for that purpose obstructing the laws for naturalization of foreigners; refusing to pass others to encourage their migrations hither, and raising the conditions of new appropriations of lands.

He has obstructed the administration of justice, by refusing his assent to laws for establishing judiciary powers.

He has made judges dependent on his will alone, for the tenure of their offices, and the amount and payment of their salaries.

He has erected a multitude of new offices, and sent hither swarms of officers to harrass our people, and eat out their substance.

He has kept among us, in times of peace, standing armies without the consent of our legislatures.

He has affected to render the military independent of and superior to the civil power.

He has combined with others to subject us to a jurisdiction foreign to our constitution, and unacknowledged by our laws; giving his assent to their acts of pretended legislation:

For quartering large bodies of armed troops among us;

For protecting them, by a mock trial, from punishment for any murders which they should commit on the inhabitants of these states;

For cutting off our trade with all parts of the world;

For imposing taxes on us without our consent;

For depriving us in many cases, of the benefits of trial by jury;

For transporting us beyond seas to be tried for pretended offenses;

For abolishing the free system of English laws in a neighboring province, establishing therein an arbitrary government, and enlarging its boundaries so as to render it at once an example and fit instrument for introducing the same absolute rule into these colonies;

For taking away our charters, abolishing our most valuable laws, and altering fundamentally the forms of our governments;

For suspending our own legislatures, and declaring themselves invested with power to legislate for us in all cases whatsoever.

He has abdicated government here, by declaring us out of his protection and waging war against us.

He has plundered our seas, ravaged our coasts, burnt our towns, and destroyed the lives of our people.

He is at this time transporting large armies of foreign mercenaries to complete the works of death, desolation and tyranny, already begun with circumstances of cruelty and perfidy scarcely paralleled in the most barbarous ages, and totally unworthy the head of a civilized nation.

He has constrained our fellow citizens taken captive on the high seas to bear arms against their country, to become the executioners of their friends and brethren, or to fall themselves by their hands.

He has excited domestic insurrections amongst us, and has endeavored to bring on the inhabitants of our frontiers, the merciless Indian savages, whose known rule of warfare, is an undistinguished destruction of all ages, sexes and conditions.

In every stage of these oppressions we have petitioned for redress in the most humble terms: our repeated petitions have been answered only by repeated injury. A prince whose character is thus marked by every act which may define a tyrant, is unfit to be the ruler of a free people.

Nor have we been wanting in attentions to our Brittish brethren. We have warned them from time to time of attempts by their legislature to extend an unwarrantable jurisdiction over us. We have reminded them of the circumstances of our emigration and settlement here. We have appealed to their native justice and magnanimity, and we have conjured them by the ties of our common kindred to disavow these usurpations, which, would inevitably interrupt our connections and correspondence. They too have been deaf to the voice of justice and of consanguinity. We must, therefore, acquiesce in the necessity, which denounces our separation, and hold them, as we hold the rest of mankind, enemies in war, in peace friends.

We, therefore, the representatives of the United States of America, in General Congress, assembled, appealing to the Supreme Judge of the world for the rectitude of our intentions, do, in the name, and by authority of the good people of these colonies, solemnly publish and declare, that these united colonies are, and of right ought to be free and independent states; that they are absolved from all allegiance to the British Crown, and that all political connection between them and the state of Great Britain, is and ought to be totally dissolved; and that as free and independent states, they have full power to levy war, conclude peace, contract alliances, establish commerce, and to do all other acts and things which independent states may of right do. And for the support of this declaration, with a firm reliance on the protection of divine providence, we mutually pledge to each other our lives, our fortunes and our sacred honor.

There are 56 signatures on the Declaration. They appear in six columns.

COLUMN 1

GEORGIA

Button Gwinnett

Lyman Hall

George Walton

COLUMN 2

NORTH CAROLINA

William Hooper

Joseph Hewes

John Penn

SOUTH CAROLINA

Edward Rutledge

Thomas Heyward, Jr.

Thomas Lynch, Jr.

Arthur Middleton

COLUMN 3

MASSACHUSETTS

John Hancock

MARYLAND

Samuel Chase

William Paca

Thomas Stone

Charles Carroll of Carrollton

VIRGINIA

George Wythe

Richard Henry Lee

Thomas Jefferson

Benjamin Harrison

Thomas Nelson, Jr.

Francis Lightfoot Lee

Carter Braxton

COLUMN 4

PENNSYLVANIA

Robert Morris

Benjamin Rush

Benjamin Franklin

John Morton

George Clymer

James Smith

George Taylor

James Wilson

George Ross

DELAWARE

Caesar Rodney

George Read

Thomas McKean

COLUMN 5

NEW YORK

William Floyd

Philip Livingston

Francis Lewis

Lewis Morris

NEW JERSEY

Richard Stockton

John Witherspoon

Francis Hopkinson

John Hart

Abraham Clark

COLUMN 6

NEW HAMPSHIRE

Josiah Bartlett

William Whipple

MASSACHUSETTS

Samuel Adams

John Adams

Robert Treat Paine

Elbridge Gerry

RHODE ISLAND

Stephen Hopkins

William Ellery

CONNECTICUT

Roger Sherman

Samuel Huntington

William Williams

Oliver Wolcott

NEW HAMPSHIRE

Matthew Thornton

Be an engaged citizen in today's world. Meet life's challenges after high school. Are you fully prepared for democratic decision making? Do you know how to address and approach issues in a democratic and responsible way? These five unique handbooks will show you how.